TODAY'S TOP DRIVERS

CHASE ELLIOTT

BY KATE MIKOLEY

Gareth Stevens PUBLISHING

HOT TOPICS

Please visit our website, www.garethstevens.com. For a free color catalog of all our high-quality books, call toll free 1-800-542-2595 or fax 1-877-542-2596.

Library of Congress Cataloging-in-Publication Data
Names: Mikoley, Kate, author.
Title: Chase Elliott / Kate Mikoley.
Description: Buffalo, N.Y. : Gareth Stevens Publishing, [2024] | Series: Today's top drivers | Includes bibliographical references and index.
Identifiers: LCCN 2023011206 | ISBN 9781538287149 (library binding) | ISBN 9781538287132 (paperback) | ISBN 9781538287156 (ebook)
Subjects: LCSH: Elliott, Chase, 1995–Juvenile literature. | Automobile racing drivers–United States–Biography–Juvenile literature. | NASCAR (Association)–Juvenile literature.
Classification: LCC GV1032.E45 M55 2024 | DDC 796.72092 [B]–dc23/eng/20230308
LC record available at https://lccn.loc.gov/2023011206

First Edition

Published in 2024 by
Gareth Stevens Publishing
2544 Clinton St
Buffalo, NY 14224

Designer: Tanya Dellaccio Keeney
Editor: Kate Mikoley

Photo credits: Series background Merydolla/Shutterstock.com; cover, pp. 1, 5, 7 (both), 9, 13 (bottom), 15, 19, 21, 23, 25 Grindstone Media Group/Shutterstock.com; pp. 11, 17 action sports/Shutterstock.com; p. 13 (top) Bristol Herald Courier/AP Images; p. 27 https://upload.wikimedia.org/wikipedia/commons/c/c7/Bill_elliott_chase_elliott_family_%2850582618917%29.jpg; p. 29 https://upload.wikimedia.org/wikipedia/commons/0/02/Chase_Elliott_Driver_Introductions_Pocono_2022.jpg.

Printed in the United States of America

CPSIA compliance information: Batch #CS24GS: For further information contact Gareth Stevens, New York, New York at 1-800-542-2595.

CONTENTS

A Popular Driver. 4
Get to Know Chase 6
Starting in NASCAR 10
Super Late Models. 12
A NASCAR Champion 14
Moving up to the Cup 16
Into the Spotlight 20
A Family Affair 26
Moving Forward. 28
Timeline 30
For More Information. 31
Glossary. 32
Index 32

A POPULAR DRIVER

There are many great race car drivers in the world. But when it comes to the most well known and loved today, one name sticks out: Chase Elliott. In fact, for five years in a row, Elliott was named NASCAR's most popular, or well-liked, driver.

IN THE FAST LANE

NASCAR stands for National Association for* Stock Car *Auto Racing. The group runs and oversees the biggest stock car races in the United States.

GET TO KNOW CHASE

Chase was born on November 28, 1995, in Dawsonville, Georgia. Many great NASCAR drivers have come from Dawsonville, such as Chase's dad, Bill Elliott. Bill won NASCAR's top **series**, the Cup Series, in 1988. He's also a member of NASCAR's Hall of Fame.

CHASE AND HIS DAD, BILL

IN THE FAST LANE

Elliott drives the No. 9 Chevrolet for Hendrick Motorsports. That's the same number his dad drove for many years.

Elliott started racing go-karts at just 8 years old. Even back then, he knew he wanted to be a NASCAR driver someday. By the time he was 15, he had driven in many types of races and had more than 60 wins.

IN THE FAST LANE

When he's not racing cars, Elliott enjoys dirt biking, snowboarding, and even flying planes!

STARTING IN NASCAR

In February 2011, Elliott got an offer to drive for a well-known NASCAR team, Hendrick Motorsports. That year, he drove in the NASCAR K&N East Series. The next year, he won his first NASCAR race at Iowa Speedway.

IN THE FAST LANE

Elliott had a driver development deal with Hendrick Motorsports. This is a kind of deal that helps young, up-and-coming drivers become great drivers for their teams.

SUPER LATE MODELS

In 2013, Elliott was racing a kind of stock car called a super late model. These are superfast cars that race on short tracks. Elliott became the first driver to win all four of the biggest super late model races.

IN THE FAST LANE

The four big super late model races Elliott won are the All-American 400, Winchester 400, World-Crown 300, and Snowball Derby.

A NASCAR CHAMPION

In 2014, Elliott made NASCAR history as the youngest person and first **rookie** to win a national series **championship**. He won the Nationwide Series, a lower level of NASCAR than the Cup Series.

IN THE FAST LANE

The Nationwide Series is now called the Xfinity Series. Many NASCAR drivers take part in the Xfinity Series before moving up to the Cup Series.

MOVING UP TO THE CUP

In 2015, the world learned that Elliott would be racing in the Cup Series the following year. To get ready, he drove in several Cup Series races in 2015. He was also racing full time in the newly renamed Xfinity Series again.

IN THE FAST LANE

Elliott came in second place in the Xfinity Series in 2015.

Once he started his first full-time season in the Cup Series, Elliott quickly made a name for himself. He became the youngest driver to win a **pole position** at the Daytona 500. He also had 10 top-five finishes that year.

IN THE FAST LANE

Elliott was Cup Series Rookie of the Year in 2016.

INTO THE SPOTLIGHT

The 2017 season was another good one for Elliott, who finished fifth in the Cup Series. However, 2018 was the year he really started to shine. It was also the year he started driving the No. 9 car, the number his father drove, in the Cup Series.

IN THE FAST LANE

While Elliott only came in sixth place in the Cup Series in 2018, he won three races and was voted most popular driver for the first time.

Elliott won most popular driver again in 2019, and yet again in 2020. That wasn't all he won in 2020. After winning the last two races in the **playoffs**, he became the winner of the Cup Series Championship!

IN THE FAST LANE

At 24 years, 11 months, and 11 days old, Elliott was the third-youngest Cup Series champion.

In both 2021 and 2022, Elliott finished in fourth place in the Cup Series. He had two wins in 2021, five in 2022, and 27 top-five finishes between the two seasons. In both years, he won most popular driver again!

IN THE FAST LANE

Elliott knows fans are important. "When there is a good crowd and people show up ... it brings a different level of ***excitement*** *to what we do and I think that rubs off on everybody," he says.*

A FAMILY AFFAIR

Chase and his dad Bill aren't the only ones in the Elliott family who are in racing. Chase's grandfather, George, owned cars that raced in NASCAR as early as the 1960s. In the 1970s, Bill started driving, with his two brothers, Ernie and Dan, working on the crew.

BILL, CHASE, AND FAMILY AT 2020 CUP SERIES

IN THE FAST LANE

Bill Elliott won 44 races during the time he was driving!

MOVING FORWARD

What's next for this accomplished driver? Perhaps one day he'll equal his father's 16 wins for most popular driver. If his past races are any sign of what's to come, we can expect lots more from this young racer!

IN THE FAST LANE

Elliott has his own foundation, or group with the goal of helping people. The Chase Elliott Foundation gives money to **charities.**

TIMELINE

NOVEMBER 28, 1995

ELLIOTT IS BORN.

2011

ELLIOTT DRIVES IN THE NASCAR K&N EAST SERIES.

2012

ELLIOTT WINS HIS FIRST NASCAR RACE.

2013

ELLIOTT BECOMES THE FIRST DRIVER TO WIN ALL FOUR BIG SUPER LATE MODEL RACES.

2014

ELLIOTT WINS THE NATIONWIDE SERIES.

2016

ELLIOTT STARTS RACING FULL-TIME IN THE CUP SERIES AND IS NAMED ROOKIE OF THE YEAR.

2018

HE WINS MOST POPULAR DRIVER FOR THE FIRST TIME.

2019

ELLIOTT WINS THE CUP SERIES CHAMPIONSHIP.

2022

HE WINS MOST POPULAR DRIVER FOR THE FIFTH YEAR IN A ROW.

FOR MORE INFORMATION

BOOKS

Cella, Clara. *Race Car Drivers*. Minneapolis, MN: Lerner Publications, 2023.

Rendle, Steve. *Race Cars*. New York, NY: PowerKids Press, 2022.

Rule, Heather. *GOATs of Auto Racing*. Minneapolis, MN: SportsZone, 2022.

WEBSITES

Chase
www.chaseelliott.com/chase
Chase Elliott's bio on his official website has more facts about him.

Chase Elliott | 9 Team
www.hendrickmotorsports.com/teams/87647/team-9
Find out more about Elliott, the car he drives, and the team he works with.

Chase Elliott NASCAR Driver Page
www.nascar.com/drivers/chase-elliott
Read more about Elliott and find his latest race stats.

GLOSSARY

championship: A contest to decide an overall winner.

charity: A group that helps those in need.

excitement: Having strong or lively feelings about something.

playoff: Having to do with races held after the regular season to decide a champion.

pole position: The best starting place for a race, determined by the fastest qualifying times.

rookie: A driver in their first year in a series.

series: A set of events or races that go together.

stock car: A racing car that looks like a regular car.

INDEX

Chase Elliott Foundation, 29
Cup Series, 6, 14, 15, 16, 18, 19, 20, 21, 22, 23, 24
Dawsonville, Georgia, 6
Daytona 500, 18
Elliott, Bill, 6, 7, 26, 27
go-kart, 8
Hendrick Motorsports, 7, 10, 11
NASCAR Hall of Fame, 6
Nationwide Series/Xfinity Series, 14, 15, 16, 17
stock car, 5, 12
super late model, 12, 13